Third Time's a Charm—Again!

Make the Most of 5" Squares with 21 Colorful Quilts

Barbara Groves and Mary Jacobson
of Me and My Sister Designs

Martingale®
Create with Confidence

Third Time's a Charm—Again!
Make the Most of 5" Squares with 21 Colorful Quilts
© 2020 by Barbara Groves and Mary Jacobson

Martingale®
19021 120th Ave. NE, Ste. 102
Bothell, WA 98011-9511 USA
ShopMartingale.com

Printed in Hong Kong
25 24 23 22 21 20   8 7 6 5 4 3 2 1

Library of Congress Cataloging-in-Publication Data is available upon request.

ISBN: 978-1-68356-104-0

MISSION STATEMENT

We empower makers who use fabric and yarn
to make life more enjoyable.

CREDITS

PUBLISHER AND
CHIEF VISIONARY OFFICER
Jennifer Erbe Keltner

CONTENT DIRECTOR
Karen Costello Soltys

DESIGN MANAGER
Adrienne Smitke

MANAGING EDITOR
Tina Cook

PRODUCTION MANAGER
Regina Girard

ACQUISITIONS AND
DEVELOPMENT EDITOR
Laurie Baker

COVER AND
BOOK DESIGNER
Mia Mar

TECHNICAL EDITOR
Ellen Pahl

PHOTOGRAPHER
Brent Kane

COPY EDITOR
Melissa Bryan

ILLUSTRATOR
Sandy Loi

Contents

Introduction

This is the fourth book in our Charm series, so it's the third time *again*! In the tradition of our previous Charm books, the quilts have been named after some of our favorite girls. Book one started with Amanda and Bertha. We've continued the theme in alphabetical order. When we ran out of letters in the alphabet, we tossed in a couple of punctuation marks for fun!

We made three quilts from every pattern in very different fabrics to show versatility. Sometimes it's difficult imagining a quilt in different fabrics so we took the extra step to show what's possible. As always, most of these quilts can be made in a day or on a weekend by an experienced quilter. Enjoy!

Barb   Mary

The Charm of Charm Squares

If you're wondering exactly what a charm square is, it's a 5" square of fabric. A charm pack is a bundle of 42 squares, 5" × 5", cut from one entire fabric collection. We love these bundles of joy because they allow us to own a square of everything in a fabric collection at an affordable price. We already know that the designer has done all the hard work of coordinating the fabrics. Our number-one tip regarding charm packs is to find one that you love. After that, anything is possible! Once you have a charm pack (and this book), the rest is easy!

That being said, though, not all charm packs are created equally. If a fabric collection is small, especially if it's a holiday-themed collection, you may receive a few repeats of some of the fabrics. Most often, the charm squares will all be different, at least in color. After we open a charm pack, we may find that there's a fabric we don't really like or there aren't enough lights or darks for the project we're making. This is when we substitute one or two squares here and there. Not every charm pack works for every project, so helping it along is not breaking any rules!

When we select a charm pack for a quilt, we often purchase the backing and binding fabrics at the same time. We'll get a few extra inches of each to use in the quilt top. That way, if there's a fabric in the charm pack that we don't like or think doesn't work in the pattern we've chosen, we substitute it with some pieces of the binding or backing fabrics—or both!

If it seems like there are too many lights or too many darks in a charm pack, or you're worried that not all of the charm squares will show up against the background, sort through the squares before sewing. While looking at the quilt assembly diagram, pair or group the light and dark squares as needed for the specific quilt. We use lots of white backgrounds in our quilts, but don't be afraid to use some color in yours. You can always make these small quilts bigger.

To ramp up the size of a quilt, purchase additional (and different) charm packs from the same designer, and you'll be able to make additional blocks for an instant scrappy quilt. If you purchase four times as many charm packs, you'll be able to make four times as many blocks.

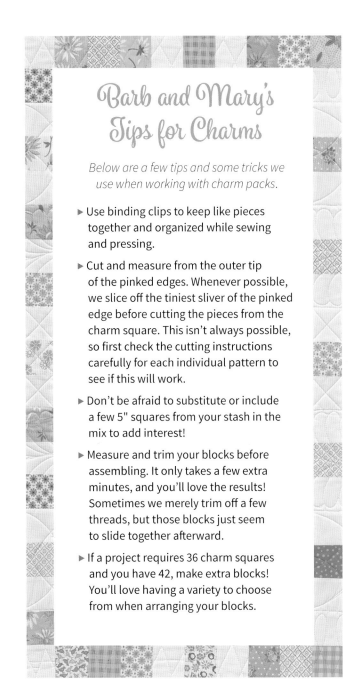

Barb and Mary's Tips for Charms

Below are a few tips and some tricks we use when working with charm packs.

► Use binding clips to keep like pieces together and organized while sewing and pressing.

► Cut and measure from the outer tip of the pinked edges. Whenever possible, we slice off the tiniest sliver of the pinked edge before cutting the pieces from the charm square. This isn't always possible, so first check the cutting instructions carefully for each individual pattern to see if this will work.

► Don't be afraid to substitute or include a few 5" squares from your stash in the mix to add interest!

► Measure and trim your blocks before assembling. It only takes a few extra minutes, and you'll love the results! Sometimes we merely trim off a few threads, but those blocks just seem to slide together afterward.

► If a project requires 36 charm squares and you have 42, make extra blocks! You'll love having a variety to choose from when arranging your blocks.

Valerie

You'll need only 36 charm squares for this cutie, so choose your favorites! While we were creating this quilt we referred to it as the PLUS sign quilt. It's the perfect candidate for making in a BIGGER version. Try using four charm packs of coordinating fabrics for four times the fun!

Finished quilt: 36½" × 36½" • Finished block: 6" × 6"

Materials

Yardage is based on 42"-wide fabric. Fabrics are from Spring Fever by Me and My Sister Designs for Moda Fabrics.

36 charm squares, 5" × 5", of assorted prints for blocks*

1¼ yards of subtle print or solid fabric for blocks

⅓ yard of fabric for binding

2½ yards of fabric for backing**

43" × 43" piece of batting

Moda charm packs contain 42 squares, 5" × 5".

**If your fabric is at least 43" wide, 1¼ yards will be enough.*

Cutting

Keep like prints together as you cut.

From *each* charm square, cut:
1 rectangle, 2½" × 4½" (36 total)
2 rectangles, 1½" × 2½" (72 total)

From the solid fabric, cut:
15 strips, 2½" × 42"; crosscut into:
- 144 squares, 2½" × 2½"
- 144 rectangles, 1½" × 2½"

From the binding fabric, cut:
4 strips, 2¼" × 42"

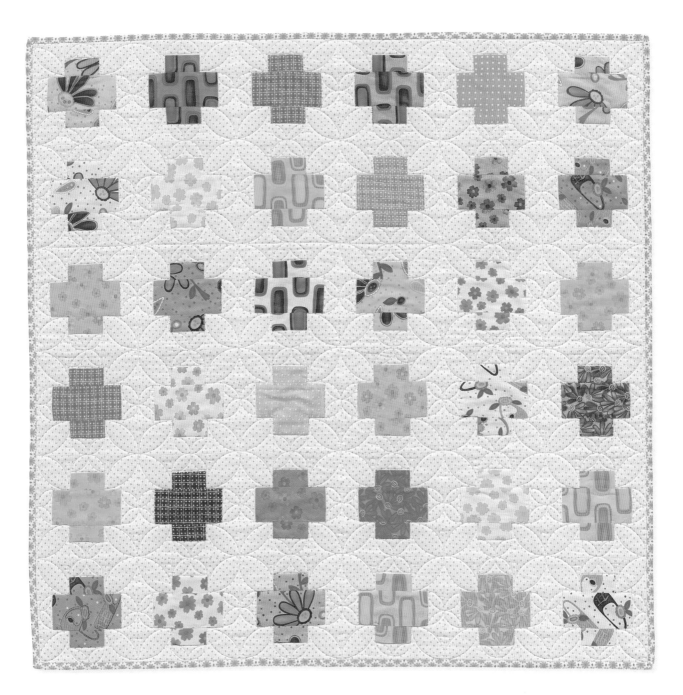

Valerie

Spring Fever fabrics by Me and My Sister Designs
take center stage in a cute plus sign quilt.

Making the Blocks

Use a ¼" seam allowance and short stitch length throughout. Press all seam allowances open. The background fabric for blocks will be referred to as "solid" in the steps.

1 Sew a print 1½" × 2½" rectangle to a solid 1½" × 2½" rectangle. Make two units that measure 2½" square, including seam allowances.

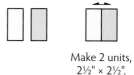

Make 2 units,
2½" × 2½".

2 Sew solid 1½" × 2½" rectangles to opposite sides of a matching print 2½" × 4½" rectangle. The unit should measure 2½" × 6½", including seam allowances.

Make 1 unit,
2½" × 6½".

3 Arrange and sew the units together with four solid 2½" squares to make the block as shown. It should measure 6½" square, including seam allowances. Make a total of 36 blocks.

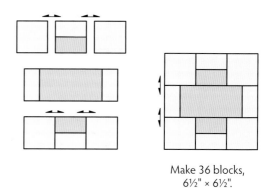

Make 36 blocks,
6½" × 6½".

Assembling the Quilt

1 Sew six blocks together to make a row that measures 6½" × 36½", including seam allowances. Make six rows.

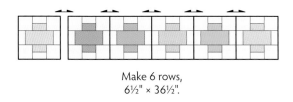

Make 6 rows,
6½" × 36½".

2 Join the rows to complete the quilt top, which should measure 36½" square.

Finishing

For more help on any of the finishing steps, go to ShopMartingale.com/HowtoQuilt for free downloadable information.

1 Layer and baste the quilt top, batting, and backing fabric.

2 Hand or machine quilt. The quilt shown is machine quilted in the ditch of the plus signs. The background features large and small pumpkin seed designs.

3 Use the 2¼" strips to make double-fold binding. Trim the excess batting and backing fabric and then attach the binding to the quilt.

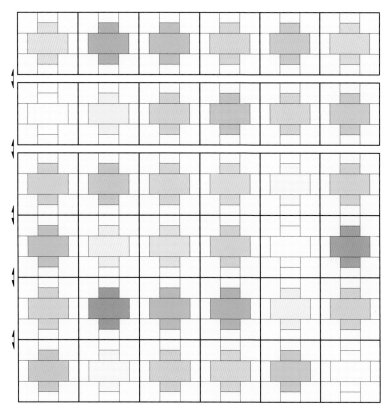

Quilt assembly

Valerie

Catalina

Featuring checks, dots, and both large- and small-scale florals, Catalina fabrics by Fig Tree & Co. add lots of charm.

Third Time's a Charm—Again!

Safari Life

Safari Life fabrics by Stacy Iest Hsu take the design in a completely new direction. Let your imagination go wild!

Whitney

You'll need 40 charm squares for this quick-and-easy quilt. Since the charm pack had 42 squares, we cut them all up and added them to the mix for variety. Sometimes we girls just gotta have more fun! Like eating potato chips, you may not want to stop with just one charm pack!

Finished quilt: 28½" × 32" • Finished block: 3" × 5½"

Materials

Yardage is based on 42"-wide fabric. Fabrics are from Back Porch by Me and My Sister Designs for Moda Fabrics.

40 charm squares, 5" × 5", of assorted prints for blocks*

¼ yard of solid fabric for blocks

⅜ yard of print fabric for border

⅓ yard of fabric for binding

1 yard of fabric for backing

33" × 36" piece of batting

Moda charm packs contain 42 squares, 5" × 5".

Cutting

From *each* charm square, cut:
3 rectangles, 1½" × 5" (120 total)

From the solid fabric, cut:
2 strips, 3½" × 42"; crosscut into 40 rectangles, 1½" × 3½"

From the print fabric, cut:
4 strips, 2½" × 42"; crosscut into:
- 2 strips, 2½" × 28"
- 2 strips, 2½" × 28½"

From the binding fabric, cut:
4 strips, 2¼" × 42"

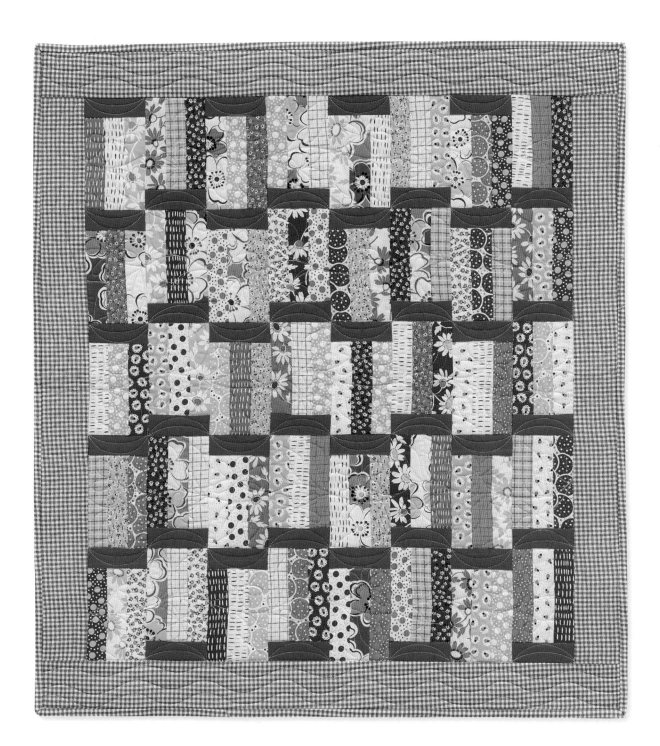

Whitney

Back Porch prints by Me and My Sister Designs
are perfect for a summertime social.

Making the Blocks

Use a ¼" seam allowance and short stitch length throughout. Press all seam allowances open.

1 Choose three assorted print 1½" × 5" rectangles for one block.

2 Sew the three print rectangles together to make a unit that measures 3½" × 5", including seam allowances.

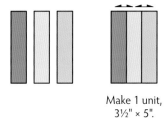

Make 1 unit,
3½" × 5".

3 Sew a solid 1½" × 3½" rectangle to one end of the unit from step 2 to make a block that measures 3½" × 6", including seam allowances. Make 40 blocks.

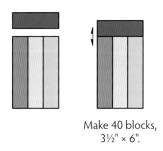

Make 40 blocks,
3½" × 6".

Assembling the Quilt

1 Sew five blocks together end to end to make a vertical row that measures 3½" × 28", including seam allowances. Make eight rows.

Make 8 rows,
3½" × 28".

2 Referring to the quilt assembly diagram, rotate every other row and join the rows to make the quilt center. It should measure 24½" × 28", including seam allowances.

Quilt assembly

3 Sew the print 2½" × 28" strips to the sides of the quilt center. Sew the print 2½" × 28½" strips to the top and bottom. The completed quilt top should measure 28½" × 32".

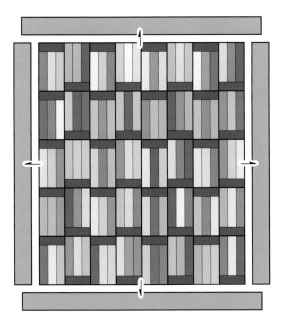

Adding borders

Finishing

For more help on any of the finishing steps, go to ShopMartingale.com/HowtoQuilt for free downloadable information.

1 Layer and baste the quilt top, batting, and backing fabric.

2 Hand or machine quilt. The quilt shown is machine quilted with flowers in the blocks, crescent moons in the solid rectangles, and wavy lines in the border.

3 Use the 2¼" strips to make double-fold binding. Trim the excess batting and backing fabric and then attach the binding to the quilt.

Whitney

Rue 1800

A soft and sweet palette gives Whitney a romantic feel with Rue 1800 fabric by 3 Sisters.

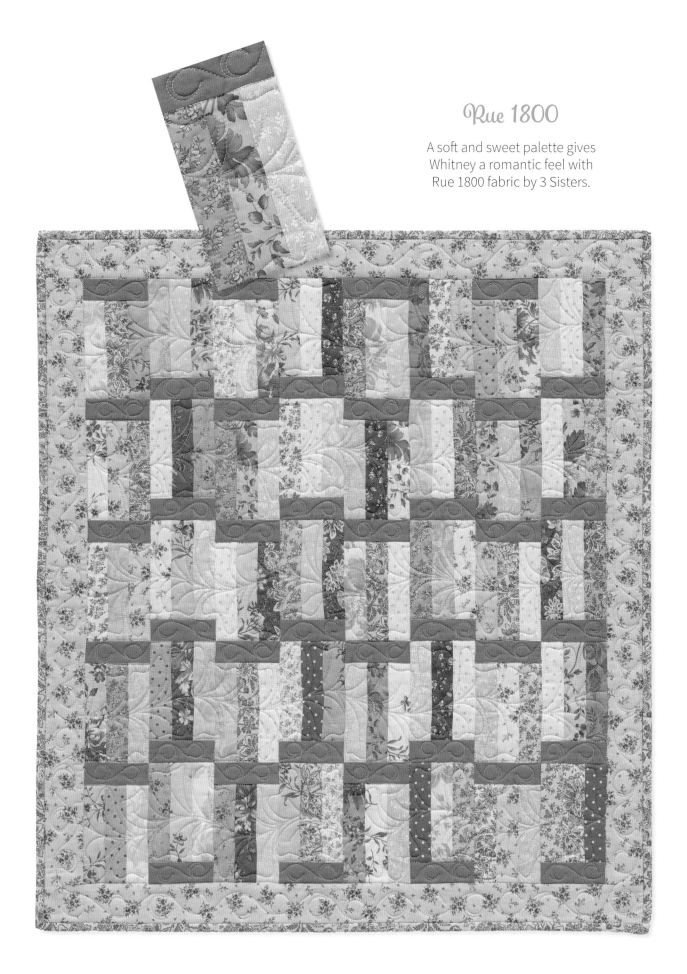

Third Time's a Charm–Again!

Breeze

The colors of sky and sea make Whitney perfect for a summer day with Breeze fabrics by Zen Chic.

Whitney

Xena

Are you feeling your inner warrior princess? There aren't many names to choose from when it comes to the letter X, but we immediately thought of the heroine from the classic fantasy television series. You'll use an entire charm pack for this project, so no leftovers. If you hate having leftovers, you'll absolutely love this quilt pattern.

Finished quilt: 38½" × 38½" • Finished block: 6" × 6"

Materials

Yardage is based on 42"-wide fabric. Fabrics are from Twirl by Me and My Sister Designs for Moda Fabrics.

42 charm squares, 5" × 5", of assorted prints for blocks*

1¼ yards of solid fabric for blocks, sashing, and border

½ yard of fabric for binding

2½ yards of fabric for backing

45" × 45" piece of batting

Moda charm packs contain 42 squares, 5" × 5".

Cutting

Divide the 42 charm squares into one stack of 25 squares and one stack of 17 squares.

From *each of the 25* charm squares, cut:
4 squares, 2½" × 2½" (100 total)

From *each of the 17* charm squares, cut:
6 squares, 1½" × 1½" (102 total; 2 are extra)

From the solid fabric, cut:
4 strips, 2" × 42"; crosscut into 100 rectangles, 1½" × 2"

4 strips, 3" × 42"; crosscut into 100 rectangles, 1½" × 3"

1 strip, 6½" × 42"; crosscut into 20 rectangles, 1½" × 6½"

4 strips, 1½" × 42"; crosscut into 4 strips, 1½" × 34½"

4 strips, 2½" × 42"; crosscut into:
  • 2 strips, 2½" × 34½"
  • 2 strips, 2½" × 38½"

From the binding fabric, cut:
5 strips, 2¼" × 42"

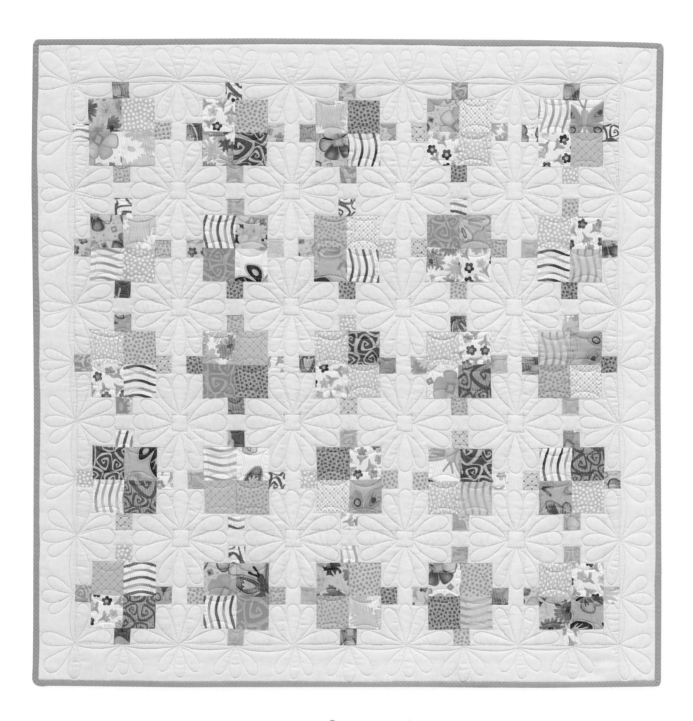

Xena

What warrior princess wouldn't love to take a whirl
with these Twirl prints by Me and My Sister Designs?

Xena

Sew a print 1½" square between two solid 1½" × 3" rectangles. Make two units that measure 1½" × 6½", including seam allowances.

Make 2 units,
1½" × 6½".

5. Arrange and sew the units together to complete a block that measures 6½" square, including seam allowances. Make 25 blocks.

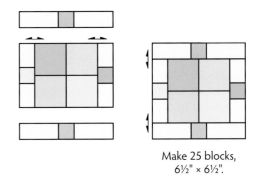

Make 25 blocks,
6½" × 6½".

Making the Blocks

Use a ¼" seam allowance and short stitch length throughout. Press all seam allowances open.

1. For each block, you will need:
   - 4 assorted print 2½" squares
   - 4 assorted print 1½" squares
   - 4 solid 1½" × 2" rectangles
   - 4 solid 1½" × 3" rectangles

2. Sew the four 2½" squares together to make a four-patch unit that measures 4½" square, including seam allowances.

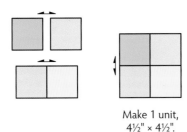

Make 1 unit,
4½" × 4½".

3. Sew a print 1½" square between two solid 1½" × 2" rectangles. Make two units that measure 1½" × 4½", including seam allowances.

Make 2 units,
1½" × 4½".

Assembling the Quilt

When adding border strips, press seam allowances away from the quilt center.

1. Sew five blocks and four solid 1½" × 6½" sashing rectangles together to make a row that measures 6½" × 34½", including seam allowances. Make five rows.

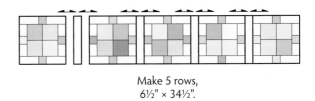

Make 5 rows,
6½" × 34½".

Third Time's a Charm–Again!

2 Join the rows and the four solid 1½" × 34½" sashing strips as shown in the quilt assembly diagram. The quilt center should measure 34½" square, including seam allowances.

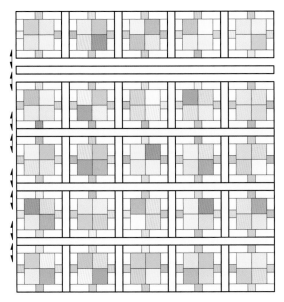

Quilt assembly

3 Sew the solid 2½" × 34½" strips to the sides of the quilt center. Sew the solid 2½" × 38½" strips to the top and bottom. The completed quilt top should measure 38½" square.

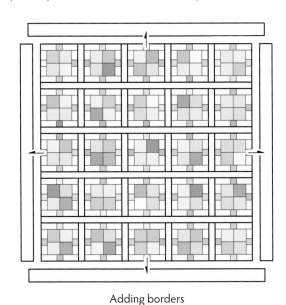

Adding borders

Finishing

For more help on any of the finishing steps, go to ShopMartingale.com/HowtoQuilt for free downloadable information.

1 Layer and baste the quilt top, batting, and backing fabric.

2 Hand or machine quilt. The quilt shown is machine quilted with large flowers between the blocks and in the border. Arcs are quilted in the block squares.

3 Use the 2¼" strips to make double-fold binding. Trim the excess batting and backing fabric and then attach the binding to the quilt.

Canning Day

We love how the varied colors and values in Canning Day fabrics by Corey Yoder add freshness and keep our eyes moving across the quilt.

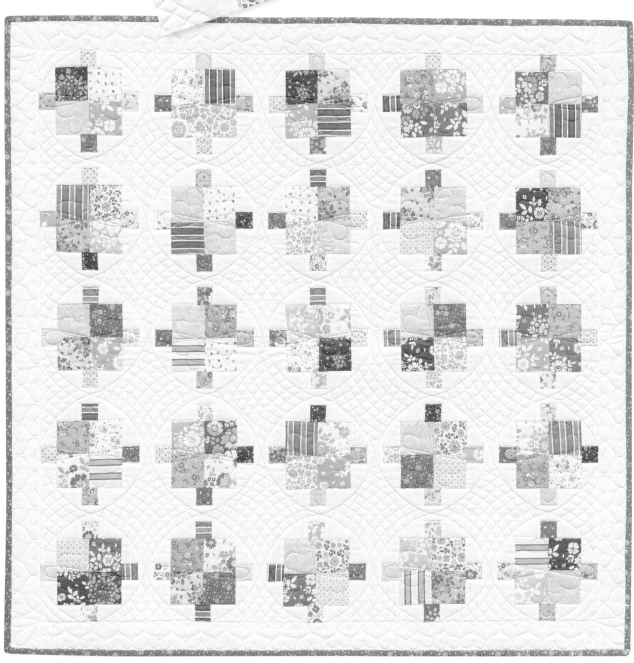

Milestones

With Milestones fabric from Kansas Troubles Quilters, warm earth tones stand out beautifully against a light background.

Xena

Yolanda

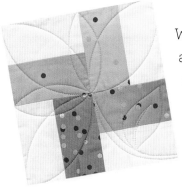

We paired up our "like" prints and kept them together to create an interesting pattern, but we have plans to make a totally random, scrappy version of this quilt someday. Rules? There are no rules! Or, if there are, we don't hesitate to break them!

Finished quilt: 32½" × 40½" • Finished block: 8" × 8"

Materials

Yardage is based on 42"-wide fabric.
Fabrics are from Ombre Confetti by V & Co.
for Moda Fabrics.

40 charm squares, 5" × 5", of assorted prints for blocks*

¾ yard of solid fabric for blocks

⅓ yard of fabric for binding**

1⅓ yards of fabric for backing

39" × 47" piece of batting

Moda charm packs contain 42 squares, 5" × 5".

**Purchase fat eighths or fat quarters in addition to charm squares if you want to make a scrappy binding.*

Cutting

Keep like prints together as you cut.

From *each* charm square, cut:
2 rectangles, 2½" × 4½" (80 total)

From the solid fabric, cut:
5 strips, 4½" × 42"; crosscut into 80 rectangles, 2½" × 4½"

From the binding fabric, cut:
4 strips, 2¼" × 42"

Yolanda

Stitched in Ombre Confetti fabrics by V & Co., the
Yolanda pattern has the look of shimmering pinwheels.

Making the Blocks

Use a ¼" seam allowance and short stitch length throughout. Press all seam allowances open.

1 Join a print and a solid 2½" × 4½" rectangle to make a unit that measures 4½" square, including seam allowances. Make 80 units.

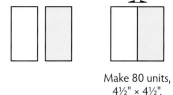

Make 80 units,
4½" × 4½".

2 Arrange and sew together four units in the same color family as shown to make a block that measures 8½" square, including seam allowances. Make a total of 20 blocks.

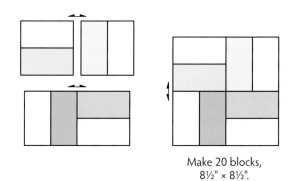

Make 20 blocks,
8½" × 8½".

Assembling the Quilt

1 Sew four blocks together to make a row that measures 8½" × 32½", including seam allowances. Make five rows.

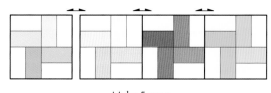

Make 5 rows,
8½" × 32½".

2 Join the rows to complete the quilt top, which should measure 32½" × 40½".

Finishing

- -

For more help on any of the finishing steps, go to ShopMartingale.com/HowtoQuilt for free downloadable information.

1 Layer and baste the quilt top, batting, and backing fabric.

2 Hand or machine quilt. The quilt shown is machine quilted with overlapping circles and leaves.

3 Use the 2¼" strips to make double-fold binding. Trim the excess batting and backing fabric and then attach the binding to the quilt.

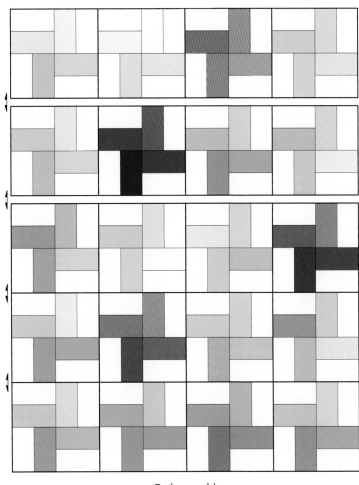

Quilt assembly

Yolanda

Sugarcreek

Like pebbles in a rippling stream, colorful prints sparkle against the blue solid with Sugarcreek by Corey Yoder.

Urban Farmhouse Gatherings

How striking Yolanda looks in neutral Urban Farmhouse Gatherings fabrics from Primitive Gatherings!

Yolanda

Zelda

If you love 2½" squares, you'll have plenty of fun making Zelda, which brings us to the final letter of the alphabet. Don't underestimate the power of simple squares and the classic Nine Patch block. We think we've saved the best for (almost) last!

Finished quilt: 34½" × 42½"
Finished blocks: 6" × 6" and 6" × 8"

Materials

Yardage is based on 42"-wide fabric. Fabrics are from Good Day by Me and My Sister Designs for Moda Fabrics.

39 charm squares, 5" × 5", of assorted prints for blocks*

1⅛ yards of solid fabric for blocks

½ yard of fabric for binding

1½ yards of fabric for backing**

41" × 49" piece of batting

Moda charm packs contain 42 squares, 5" × 5".

**If your fabric isn't at least 41" wide, you'll need 2¼ yards to piece the backing horizontally.*

Cutting

From *each* charm square, cut:
4 squares, 2½" × 2½" (156 total; 3 are extra)

From the solid fabric, cut:
13 strips, 2½" × 42"; crosscut into:
- 28 rectangles, 2½" × 8½"
- 8 rectangles, 2½" × 6½"
- 68 squares, 2½" × 2½"

From the binding fabric, cut:
5 strips, 2¼" × 42"

Zelda

Zelda sure is cheerful stitched from Good Day
prints by Me and My Sister Designs.

Making the Blocks

Use a ¼" seam allowance and short stitch length throughout. Press all seam allowances open.

1 Arrange and sew four assorted print 2½" squares together with two solid 2½" × 8½" rectangles to make block A as shown. Make 14 blocks that measure 6½" × 8½", including seam allowances.

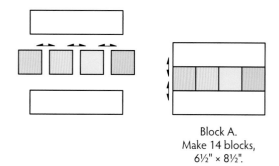

Block A.
Make 14 blocks,
6½" × 8½".

2 Arrange and sew three assorted print 2½" squares together with two solid 2½" × 6½" rectangles to make block B as shown. Make four blocks that measure 6½" square, including seam allowances.

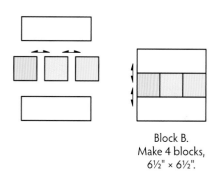

Block B.
Make 4 blocks,
6½" × 6½".

3 Arrange and sew five assorted print 2½" squares together with four solid 2½" squares to make a Nine Patch block as shown. Make 17 blocks that measure 6½" square, including seam allowances.

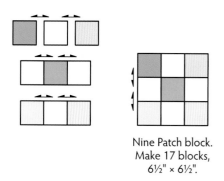

Nine Patch block.
Make 17 blocks,
6½" × 6½".

Assembling the Quilt

1 Arrange and sew two A blocks, one B block, and two Nine Patch blocks into a row that measures 6½" × 34½", including seam allowances. Make four rows.

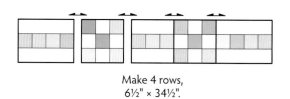

Make 4 rows,
6½" × 34½".

Third Time's a Charm—Again!

2 Arrange and sew three Nine Patch blocks and two A blocks into a row that measures 6½" × 34½", including seam allowances. Make three rows.

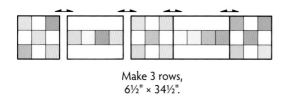

Make 3 rows,
6½" × 34½".

3 Referring to the quilt assembly diagram, alternate the rows and then join them to complete the quilt top, which should measure 34½" × 42½".

Finishing

For more help on any of the finishing steps, go to ShopMartingale.com/HowtoQuilt for free downloadable information.

1 Layer and baste the quilt top, batting, and backing fabric.

2 Hand or machine quilt. The quilt shown is machine quilted with different patterns across the rows, including loops, cables, and feathers. The center block row is quilted in a diagonal grid.

3 Use the 2¼" strips to make double-fold binding. Trim the excess batting and backing fabric and then attach the binding to the quilt.

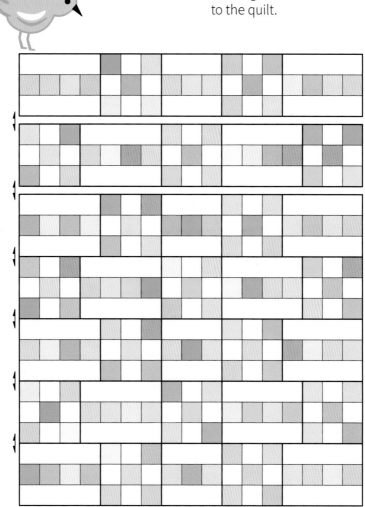

Quilt assembly

Zelda

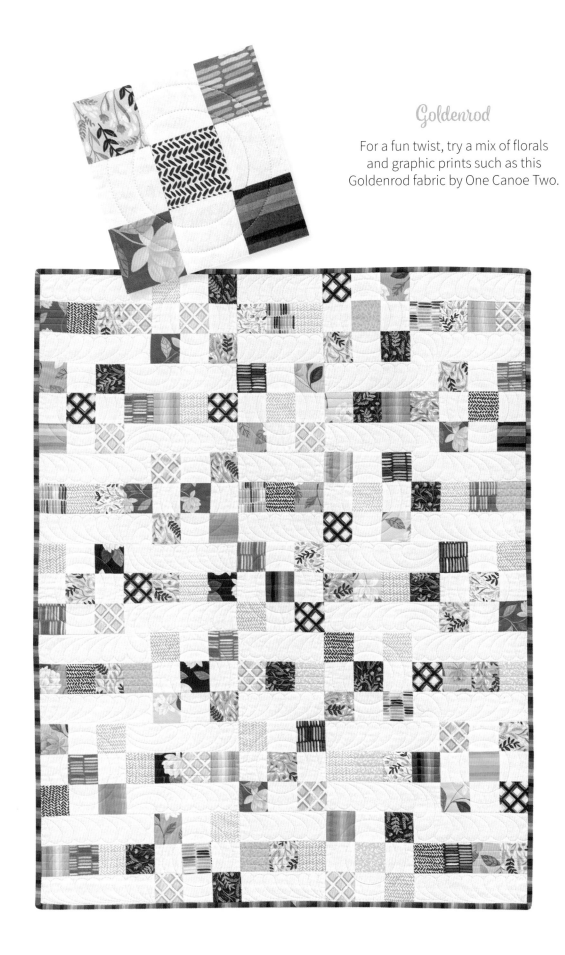

Goldenrod

For a fun twist, try a mix of florals and graphic prints such as this Goldenrod fabric by One Canoe Two.

Finnegan

Finnegan by Brenda Riddle shows
Zelda in quiet lavenders and greens
for a lovely, restful quilt.

Zelda

Exclamation Point!

Having reached the end of the alphabet, we resorted to using punctuation marks to name the last two quilts! Cutting a charm square in half diagonally and inserting a solid strip changes everything, opening up all sorts of possibilities. We think this is the most unusual setting in the book and deserves an exclamation point! Feel free to play with the blocks as you lay them out to create your own unique arrangement.

Finished quilt: 33½" × 38" • Finished block: 4½" × 4½"

Materials

Yardage is based on 42"-wide fabric. Fabrics are from Bubble Pop by Sandy Klop of American Jane.

42 charm squares, 5" × 5", of assorted prints for blocks*

⅝ yard of solid fabric for blocks

½ yard of print for border

⅓ yard of fabric for binding

1¼ yards of fabric for backing

40" × 44" piece of batting

Moda charm packs contain 42 squares, 5" × 5".

Cutting

Keep like prints together as you cut.

Cut *each* charm square in half diagonally to make:

2 triangles (84 total)

From the solid fabric, cut:
2 strips, 8½" × 42"; crosscut into 42 strips, 1½" × 8½"

From the border fabric, cut:
4 strips, 3½" × 42"; crosscut into:
- 2 strips, 3½" × 32"
- 2 strips, 3½" × 33½"

From the binding fabric, cut:
4 strips, 2¼" × 42"

Exclamation Point!

Bubble Pop prints from American Jane
are so worthy of an exclamation point!

Making the Blocks

Use a ¼" seam allowance and short stitch length throughout. Press all seam allowances open.

1 Fold two matching triangles and a solid 1½" × 8½" strip in half to find the centers; crease.

2 Aligning the centers, sew the strip between the two triangles to make a block. Trim the block to measure 5" square. Make 42 blocks.

Assembling the Quilt

When adding borders, press seam allowances away from the quilt center.

1 Arrange and sew seven rows of six blocks each, orienting the blocks as shown in the quilt assembly diagram. Sew the rows together to make the quilt center, which should measure 27½" × 32", including seam allowances.

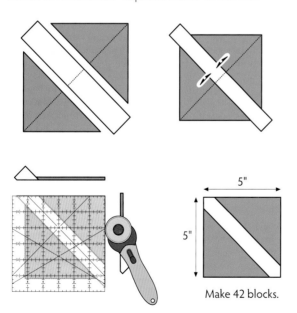

Make 42 blocks.

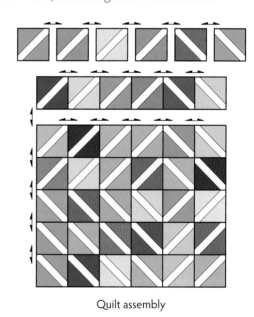

Quilt assembly

2 Sew the 3½" × 32" border strips to the sides of the quilt center. Sew the 3½" × 33½" border strips to the top and bottom. The completed quilt top should measure 33½" × 38".

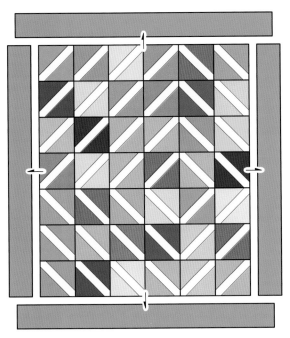

Adding borders

Finishing

For more help on any of the finishing steps, go to ShopMartingale.com/HowtoQuilt for free downloadable information.

1 Layer and baste the quilt top, batting, and backing fabric.

2 Hand or machine quilt. The quilt shown is machine quilted with crescents in the triangles and a line of circles in the strips.

3 Use the 2¼" strips to make double-fold binding. Trim the excess batting and backing fabric and then attach the binding to the quilt.

Ticklish

Exclamation Point! is oh-so pink and pretty with Ticklish fabric by Me and My Sister Designs.

Third Time's a Charm–Again!

Scarlet and Sage

Gorgeous florals and low-contrast diagonals create a rich look with Scarlet and Sage fabric by Fig Tree & Co.

Question Mark?

There's no question in our minds that this was our favorite quilt to make. Simple construction results in kite-shaped Pinwheel blocks that look much more complex than they are. Pinwheels rule, right?

Finished quilt: 36½" × 44½" • Finished block: 8" × 8"

Materials

Yardage is based on 42"-wide fabric. Fabrics are from Flour Garden by Linzee Kull McCray for Moda Fabrics.

40 charm squares, 5" × 5", of assorted prints for blocks*

1⅓ yards of solid fabric for blocks and border

½ yard of fabric for binding

2⅞ yards of fabric for backing**

43" × 51" piece of batting

*Moda charm packs contain 42 squares, 5" × 5".

**If your fabric is at least 43" wide, 1½ yards will be enough.

Cutting

Keep like prints together as you cut.

From the solid fabric cut:

5 strips, 5" × 42"; crosscut into 40 squares, 5" × 5"

4 strips, 2" × 42"; crosscut into 80 squares, 2" × 2"

4 strips, 2½" × 42"; crosscut into:
- 2 strips, 2½" × 40½"
- 2 strips, 2½" × 36½"

From the binding fabric, cut:

5 strips, 2¼" × 42"

Question Mark?

No question about it, pinwheels stitched in
Flour Garden by Linzee Kull McCray are delightful!

Making the Blocks

Use a ¼" seam allowance and short stitch length throughout. Press all seam allowances open.

1 Draw a diagonal line from corner to corner on the wrong side of each solid 5" square.

2 With right sides facing, layer a marked solid square with a print 5" square. Stitch ¼" from each side of the drawn line. Cut along the line and press open to make two half-square-triangle units. Trim the units to measure 4½" square. Make a total of 80 units.

Make 80 units.

3 Draw a diagonal line from corner to corner on the wrong side of each solid 2" square.

4 With right sides facing, layer a marked 2" square on one corner of each half-square-triangle unit as shown. Stitch on the drawn line. Trim the seam allowances to ¼". Flip and press. Repeat for each of the 80 half-square-triangle units.

Make 80 units,
4½" × 4½".

5 Arrange and sew four half-square-triangle units into a Pinwheel block. Make 20 blocks that measure 8½" square, including seam allowances. Feel free to use four different units in each block, as we did, or two each of two matching units, as in the quilt shown on page 46.

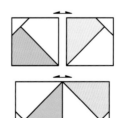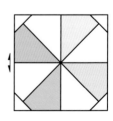

Make 20 blocks,
8½" × 8½".

Third Time's a Charm–Again!

Assembling the Quilt

1 Sew four blocks together to make a row that measures 8½" × 32½", including seam allowances. Make five rows.

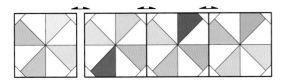

Make 5 rows,
8½" × 32½".

2 Join the rows to make the quilt center, which should measure 32½" × 40½", including seam allowances.

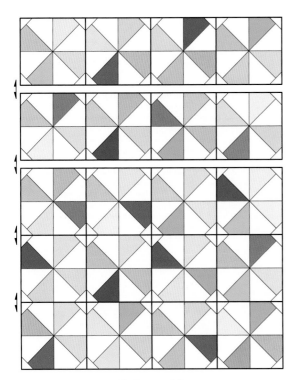

Quilt assembly

3 Sew the solid 2½" × 40½" strips to the sides of the quilt center. Sew the solid 2½" × 36½" strips to the top and bottom. The completed quilt top should measure 36½" × 44½".

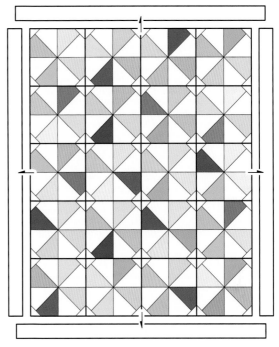

Adding borders

Finishing

For more help on any of the finishing steps, go to ShopMartingale.com/HowtoQuilt for free downloadable information.

1 Layer and baste the quilt top, batting, and backing fabric.

2 Hand or machine quilt. The quilt shown is machine quilted with squared-off leaves in the solid areas and closely spaced parallel lines in the prints.

3 Use the 2¼" strips to make double-fold binding. Trim the excess batting and backing fabric and then attach the binding to the quilt.

Question Mark?

Fiddle Dee Dee

Like brightly colored candy in a gleaming white dish, the design is irresistible with Fiddle Dee Dee fabric by Me and My Sister Designs.

Abby Rose

With Abby Rose fabrics by Robin Pickens, we love how the orange adds vibrancy and works so well with the pinks, greens, and bold blues.

Acknowledgment

The very talented Sharon Elsberry, whose business is called Akamai Quilts, machine quilted all the quilts in this book.

About the Authors

Sisters Barbara Groves and Mary Jacobson make up the popular design team of Me and My Sister Designs, based in Tempe, Arizona. Their belief in fast, fun, and easy designs can be seen in the quilts created for their pattern company, in their books, and in their fabric designs for Moda. To learn more, visit the authors at MeandMySisterDesigns.com.